# Who Are You?

For Thoughtful People, Who Are Curious About Creating a Life of Awareness.

Felicity Green

Balboa Press books may be ordered through booksellers or by contacting:

Balboa Press
A Division of Hay House
1663 Liberty Drive
Bloomington, IN 47403
www.balboapress.com
1 (877) 407-4847

ISBN: 978-1-5043-6953-4 (sc)
ISBN: 978-1-5043-6954-1 (e)

Library of Congress Control Number: 2016919752

Print information available on the last page.

Balboa Press rev. date: 07/19/2017

BALBOA
PRESS
A DIVISION OF HAY HOUSE

*Dedicated to my mother and father who gave my life to me.*

*And my spiritual mother and father*

*who gave me a path to wisdom.*

# *Acknowledgements*

    This book would never have been written without the support of my eldest son Steven. I live on a fixed income, had the book in mind but felt I didn't have the extra money to write it. He persuaded me I could get donations from Indiegogo. I did and was able to complete this book due to the generosity of too many people to name. Once I had decided to write the book and had started I had a friend Darlene Dibble offer to help. That friendly support was so valuable to get me going. After a while Nina Rook a former student phoned me and said she had heard I was writing a book and offered to read and edit it. What another wonderful offer hers was. Gary Transue, a former student and longtime close friend, read an early addition and gave important suggestions that helped with the overall flow of the book. I have been so fortunate to have these generous friends who gave their time and efforts. Lastly my assistant, Liz Lafferty, has been the most outstanding help in bringing the book to its last form. Not only the writing, but the design. She poked and prodded me, often to expand my writing. Without the many donations from friends and supporters, throughout the two years I would have not been able to do this. So there are many people in the background to whom I am eternally grateful. This book is my legacy to the next generations. I know we all have to invent the wheel, but suggestions and inspiration can help.

*Blessings*

FelicityGreenYoga.com

I'd like to thank and acknowledge the sources of a few of the special pictures in this book.

Pg. 28  The BOUNTY Project ©

Pg. 60 The Cedar Grove © Steve Horn

Back Cover picture of Felicity © Steve Horn

# Table of Contents

# Preface

I am a woman in my 82<sup>nd</sup> year who has practiced a particular discipline for 50 years.

This book is not about that discipline, it is about the benefit of having a daily practice. Having had a daily practice that I have stayed true to for all these years, I feel I have made progress in understanding myself, and in being comfortable in my own skin.

I am writing a book that I hope is thoughtful, encouraging and inspiring while at the same time practical. My intention is to share the occasions of learning that have helped me on my journey, hopefully pointing you toward finding a practice that works for you.

I am not advocating a particular practice. We are all unique and there are many practices or paths that may suit you. My advice is to choose carefully and go deeply into it. The secret of evolving is developing awareness.

For me the everyday world of children, friends, challenges and failures has been the avenue through which I have learned to become aware and more engaged in the present.

*"A life unexamined is a life not worth living."* Voltaire

As a young woman I lived my life on the surface, flitting from thing to thing, everything to me was superficial. I felt there were too many things to take care of. I felt overloaded, tired and desperate. Then I created space and time for myself, which to most would appear selfish. But the commitment to myself was of ultimate importance to me. I discovered that it enhanced my relationships and it created for me a depth of understanding that I had not had before. So life became calmer and I felt more able to deal with everything. Though the lessons have not always been easy or pleasant, I believe my spirit was embodied so that I could live a full life and face challenges in a way that would help me evolve. I have understood it is my responsibility to respond with the best awareness and tools I know at the time. As I evolved my daily external life changed. I know there will always be pain and pleasure—that is life, I experience them and try to allow them to flow by like a leaf on a river. Suffering, however, is the mental continuation of pain. That is where my life has changed. My practices have helped me to develop wisdom with less self-inflicted suffering.

*"Pain is inevitable. Suffering is optional."*
*Haruki Murakami*

My practice created the quiet space in my busy life and connected me to my deeper true self, giving me a center to live my life in accordance with my beliefs.

In my eyes, an authentic person is someone who is comfortable in their skin, knows about themselves on many levels, and is always ready to move out of old habits and accept challenges with new responses.

Speaking in generalities now, biologically our eyes create a certain attitude to life. As women we are generalists and see broadly. One of the reasons being our eye structure which has more cones than rods, the shape of the cells allows us see the big picture. Men are more inclined to see the smaller details as biologically they have more rods than cones in their eyes. Women need to learn to focus and men need to broaden their vision to see the bigger picture.

To women, the world and nature is our learning ground, so it is often the ordinary, the small things in life, in which we discover how to transform ourselves.

My insights into myself came through many avenues, such as my children and family life, my partners, my friends, my work, adventure and travel; and most importantly my belief in Yoga Ethics. As the Buddhists say, it is for women to learn skillful action, and for men it is to learn compassion.

Focusing for women is difficult, particularly in the childrearing years. But when I decided I really wanted to focus I found I could free up the necessary space in my life for practice.

My path to discipline and focus has been through Iyengar Yoga. Iyengar taught traditionally based on Pathanjali's Sutras. The yoga term "darshana" is often translated in English as "philosophy", but it means, "the way to live your life ethically." As my practice, which I started in 1964, deepened, my daily life changed to become more in line with Yoga Ethics. Patanjali is said to be someone who lived 7000 years ago in India and wrote about the human condition.

I believe our daily life is inseparable from our spiritual life. The way I live my life must be in accordance with my beliefs. Connecting to my God-Essence every day in my practice and quiet time nurtures my Being. If your practice does not affect your daily life on a deep level it has only superficial meaning. I believe life is like a school. I have a human existence to face challenges as opportunities to learn about myself, to refine my Spirit and to be true to myself. Even events which appear negative most often have a gem of learning in them, and it is my responsibility to seek out the gem in each event.

My practices have helped me to develop wisdom so that I am able to live a life with less self-inflicted suffering. I know there will always be pain and pleasure but these are fleeting, whereas suffering is a mental replay of past pain. When we bring a painful memory back or project pain into the future we are inflicting suffering upon ourselves.

I have learned it is my choice what attitude I choose to take in different circumstances. This ability to choose has become increasingly under my control. I can decide to be happy or unhappy, accepting or rejecting, rigid or flexible. I take more time to check that my intention is congruent with mind and heart, and I recognizing when these aspects are in agreement, and I can confidently make a choice even if it means letting go of a sense of security.

For me this book is a regenerative action of handing down hard won insights. I'm sharing the things that helped me. You'll have to find your own way: what practice and what exercises work for you and help you to discover your deeper nature.

Blessings,
Felicity Green

## An Important PS

To learn the most about yourself, I recommend you personalize each quote. As I did in my journey, replace the words "You," "Yourself," "we," or "one," with "I" and "Myself." This will help you to see if you are meeting the challenge.

*"I don't know whether the universe, with its countless galaxies,*

*stars and planets has a deeper meaning or not,*

*but at the very least, it is clear*

*that we humans who live on this earth face the task*

*of making a happy life for ourselves.*

*Therefore, it is important to discover what*

*will bring about the greatest degree of happiness."*

His Holiness the Dalai Lama

# Introduction

*"Learn to cooperate with your own evolution and then you won't be hit by a 2x4."*
Swami Shivananda Radha

A 2x4 is when the Universe creates a big lesson, an accident, a fall, or some such thing to wake you up.

s a teacher I have been a communicator. As I no longer travel and teach, I missed the communication and decided a book was the way to go. My discipline has helped me to reach a place of grace and ease in my life. This is what I want to share.

This is not a book about a particular practice. It is the many sips of honey I have experienced that have helped me to reach a place of being that is joyful and remains creative.

I hope this book will be an inspiration to others. I am an ordinary human being, but I have garnered wisdom, humor, and compassion through my experiences.

As a child I grew up in a doctor's family. My Grandfather and Father were General Practioners as they were called then, and my Mother was a nurse. My father was an old fashioned family doctor who visited his patients in their home if there was any hint of a fever, infection or a handicap. Because of this, my father knew the families and their circumstances.

As a child I was very shy. I can remember when meeting unknown people I would turn and bury my head in my mother's skirt. I grew up with two older brothers who were disabled and a younger sister. As a family, we were always looked at, which for me created great embarrassment. I frequently felt a longing to disappear into the background. My eldest brother had a clubbed foot. The younger brother had a form of dwarfism. As my sister was five and a half years younger, as children it was almost as though we were of a different generation.

As I grew up, wondering why they had handicaps and I apparently had none, created in me curiosity about life's seemingly unjust circumstances. In my teenage years I asked many questions of people who I thought would be wise in the ways of God. I ask Priests and Ministers why my brothers were born with these obstacles to a normal life, and not me? I never got an answer except that they were unlucky and I was not. To me this made life seem like a lottery. I have always felt that life had a purpose and that it should be logical and follow laws and not be random.

*Time*
*has a wonderful way of*
*showing us*
*what really matters.*

After high school I trained as an Occupational Therapist which required doing the first two years of medical training including one year of dissection of a human body from skin level to bone.

When I worked, it was both in the physical and psychological fields. From these experiences I realized that while the physical aspect was important for a healthy life, so was the mental aspect, our thoughts and feelings being the Creator of our lives.

I married in 1956 and started a family, and that became my focus. But the political situation in South Africa was deteriorating and the police had fired on black protestors for the first time. I didn't want to bring up my children amidst the hatred and violence of Apartheid. In 1962 I had the courage to leave close friends and family to make a move from South Africa to America. I flew to New York and then California, where my husband had been hired by Stanford Research Institute. I was alone on a 24 hour flight with three small boys – four years old, two years old and a three month old baby.

*"Every now and then doing something crazy prevents permanent insanity."*

Liz Lafferty

Upon my arrival I landed with three small children and had no one to greet me. I was helped in New York by a black porter – inconceivable in Apartheid South Africa. He helped me to change buses to the other terminal. He gave me American money to phone my husband in California. He showed me how to use the phone. And at his suggestion he watched the children while I spoke to my husband. He was a black angel and I regret to this day that I didn't give him a substantial tip as recognition of his kindness and generosity, as I felt he saved my life.

My experiences of taking what appeared to others to be crazy choices, have been the most life-changing and rewarding.

The adjustment to a different way of life was extremely stressful. I had shoulder reconstruction six months before leaving South Africa because I had a chronic dislocation of my left shoulder. The prognosis indicated that I would never get full movement in that shoulder. Having three young boys and a bum shoulder, help was essential. In South Africa I had a maid to help me. With the move and change in money values we simply didn't have the funds to hire help, so I struggled on.

I started Yoga to see how much movement I could regain, it took 10 years to eventually have full movement in my shoulders. The surprise that came-- and kept me going, was a rapid psychological result along with the slow physical improvement. I gradually felt more grounded and able to cope. As the children were still small, I found out the best solution was for me to climb into the playpen to do Yoga and let the kids run around in the room.

A few years later, I was introduced to the book "Many Mansions" by Gina Ceriminara. It tells the story of Edgar Cayce, the Sleeping Prophet, who lived in Virginia Beach in the early twentieth century. He believed in reincarnation, a theory I had heard about but knew nothing of its meaning. This understanding of life and the reasons why we might come into this life with challenges that we have to face was very exciting to me. It made sense and so became my belief system. Reincarnation is a belief that is held by many prominent Westerners as well as East Indians. It explains to me geniuses like Mozart who start producing works of music at a very young age.

Many children will tell you that their name is something other than what their family calls them, or that they live somewhere else. In western beliefs this is "child's play", imagination, foolishness. In India, where people believe in reincarnation, stories told by children are accepted as past life recollections. Many of these stories have been checked out and consistently prove to be true.

Swami Radha said we come into this world with 50% already there. Consider babies, in my case now four boys born to the same parents, yet I observed they were unique in their reactions from the minute they were born.

In 1981 with the boys grown, I went to Yasodhara Ashram, in British Columbia to study with Swami Radha. After three years, I left the ashram and moved to Seattle with all my possessions in my little Mazda car.

Two years later I listened to my dreams, and in 1987, bought property on Lopez Island off the coast of Washington State. An exquisite property with a lovely cedar grove, it quite literally fell into my hands. Trusting my intuitive feelings I was able to make a decision that seemed foolish to the logical brain, leaping into developing a Summer Yoga Retreat center.

I feel that human beings have freedom of choice in how we live and behave. We can choose to have a life that is ethical and responsible, or we can remain ignorant, dull and undeveloped. We can either live out our fate or take courage and live out our destiny. My choice for my life has been to get to know myself, to develop my awareness and to live ethically. Once I decided on a direction for myself decisions came more easily. I would ask myself the question, "Is my choice taking me in the direction I have chosen or is it not?"

My path has been the practice of Iyengar Yoga with B.K.S. Iyengar and Kundalini Yoga with Swami Radha, my root teachers. Through the grace of personal study with these two teachers, I was introduced to a world beyond previous knowing. I began to see the connection between disciplines of the body and disciplines of the mind. For instance, non-violence, honesty and the other eight ethical disciplines can be learned through the body. I learned that creating space in my body created space mentally as well. I read broadly and attended many varied workshops, all conscious choices to stay with my path to evolve as a human being. It's easy to make these simple sentences on paper, but in life courage and will are always necessary to face challenges.

East Indians often visualize an image of a crystal. It has many facets and may have flaws, but it is clear and beautiful. In fact the flaws give it its character and beauty. None of us is perfect, as this is the human condition. When I face and acknowledge my shadow "flaws" and do not use my imperfections as excuses I become richer and more authentic.

## 10 Disciplines of Yoga

Non-Violence

Non-Lying

Moderation

Non-Stealing

Non-Coveting

Cleanliness

Contentment

Effort

Self-Study

Belief in a

Higher Power

During my life I have found harmony and life has felt like heaven, a time of great awareness and joy. But I have also had occasions to drop to the bottom and be in despair. Each of these ascents and descents has been an opportunity for learning and growth. Often in the 20/20 vision of looking back I can see that even those apparently negative experiences were all part of my evolution. I feel there is still an area of myself that I don't fully know, there to be explored with courage and awareness.

So, life continues to be an adventure.

Yoga Asanas taught me that by creating space in my body I created space in my mind and my life.

I will be using quotes, parables and stories throughout the book. This is the honey I have taken from many sources of the Perennial Philosophy which is present at the deepest level of all religious and spiritual endeavors.

Yoga has been my root discipline, but the flowers of wisdom have arisen from many ages and cultures. It is not enough just to read and agree with wisdom, rather it is necessary to take action to bring these principles into being or else it is simply intellectual data. It is only when you take action and experience it that you're able to say you know.

This book is purposefully written to be full of challenges. Though I could have written it all as a memoir, it would be too easy for you, the reader, to distance yourself.

*"To develop character and wisdom and cultivate our spiritual nature we must create a balance and integration between the external and internal within ourselves."*

Rumi

## A BUSHMAN SAYING

*They say there is a physical hunger, what they call*

*the Greatest Hunger,*

*that is the hunger for meaning.*

*There is only one thing that is insufferable and that is*

*life without meaning.*

*There is nothing wrong with the search for happiness,*

*but there is something great*

*in meaning*

*which transfigures all.*

*When you have meaning you are content,*

*you belong.*

*Sir Laurens van der Post*

# Chapter 1

# The Well

*"This is a story of two men that go to look for a place to dig a well for water. One man stays digging in the same place and at the end of the week has found water. The other man kept doubting himself and moved every half day and ended up with fourteen shallow holes and no water."*

*An Old East Indian Story*

The metaphor of digging the well continues on through the process of learning about yourself. The depth of the well is in a sense the depth that you understand yourself. As your life is changing, as you grow older and evolve, your outer and inner challenges will be changing. Just as a well has to be periodically checked and cleaned you revisit the well and make sure the water of life is still flowing clearly and beautifully.

You usually realize you want to become more aware about yourself because something in your life is uncomfortable physically or emotionally. This is a prod from the Universe to become curious, courageous and committed to helping yourself. Often difficulties turn out to be blessings because they encourage you to face your fears and limitations.

The work of digging into yourself is to be radically honest with yourself about daily life, about your relationships with family, friends, and society and about your relationship to yourself. You must be radically honest both in your rational mind and in your emotional gut. Working in this way clarifies your motives for change. When complete honesty about the truth of your life occurs in your mind and gut, there is an unmistakable resolution to the problem you are grappling with.

Six weeks before leaving South Africa I had an operation for a chronic shoulder injury. The prognosis for recovery was not good and I was told I would never lift my elbow above my shoulder again. After a year in the USA I saw an advertisement in a local paper for a yoga class and thought this might help me to get movement back into my shoulder, which is why I started my discipline. It took ten years to get full movement back into the shoulder joint. Although I thought I was doing a physical practice, during that time I learned a lot about myself.

I started Yoga because of the calamity of a painful shoulder, that calamity led me to Yoga, which led me into a daily practice, which unfolded into a teaching life. For about three years I had practiced on the lawn at my home every morning. A friend asked if she could join me. I said sure. She did. And several weeks she said she had a couple of friends who were also interested. I had studied from books and gone to workshops, so I felt I knew a little and corrected them as I could. This was how I was led into being a Yoga teacher: because the number of students kept growing.

Accepting challenges and nudges from your life are the jewels to help you discover yourself.

Are you willing to make space in your outer life for this adventure? Say you have decided to practice in the morning before your outer life begins. You will have to sacrifice your time in bed, reading the newspaper or whatever your usual morning ritual is. You may prefer to have your practice time later in the day. You have to make the decision how to best fit it in with your schedule.

Personally, I have always felt that the early morning practice creates a center for yourself and your day then evolves from this centered place.

So let's start digging. This is the surface. You are looking at the relationships that you have with society, your family and yourself. Observe if you have any difficulties in any of these areas.

The ground could be soft and easy to work with, or it may be hard and rocky. Looking at yourself honestly is the first breakthrough. Are you aware of the masks that you put on to face the world? You may have different masks for different situations, for example, are you wearing the soft pliable mask or the strong tough mask? You have been through many phases in your lifetime and may have developed ways of being which have become habitual. For instance are these childhood habits, which were often survival techniques, appropriate or useful at this present time?

As you continue with your practice, digging deeper you will have times when it is easy going and you may think that that this is as far as you have to go. Or, you may experience times when it is hard and you are struggling to move forward. Life will tell you it you need to go further.

If the ground is hard, what would you use to soften it? Water? Water is a gentle element and yet very powerful. It created the Grand Canyon, but it took time; sometimes great patience is needed. There are times when the water will follow a natural path and you can relax and flow with the river; it flows by itself.

**Sometimes you need to:**

*"Be soft in your practice,*

*Think of it as a fine silvery steam,*

*Not a raging waterfall.*

*Follow the stream,*

*Have faith in its course.*


*It will go its own way*

*Meandering here,*

*Trickling there.*

*It will find the grooves,*

*The cracks, the crevices.*

*Just follow it.*

*Never let it out of your sight.*

*It will take you."*

-Sheng-yen.

Now, to return to the analogy of the well, there are also times in your journey when you have to blast. These are the old stories you have told yourself that have hardened with time into rock. It's not wrong to have stories, we all have them. It's when you cling to those of your stories that are not true, that they harden and limit your life.

I have always thought of myself as having a fear of heights. This started when I was 5 years old visiting Botswana with my family. We had to cross a bridge that was made of planks with spaces of 2 inches. I was terrified and carefully stepped on each plank convinced I could easily fall through the spaces. This continued into my mid-life, carefully stepping over the gap in the front of an elevator. Still believing my story, whenever I was in a high place I stayed far from the edge. Then in my fifties I was on the trek in Nepal and came to the first suspension bridge. I sat down thinking I could go no further. A yak driver came along shouting and throwing stones at his ten yaks to make them cross the bridge and they pounded their way over. I realized that if the bridge could stand that it would be safe for me to cross. The rock of my story began to crack. I met many more suspension bridges and scary trails in Nepal and with each crossing the hard fixed perception of my old story about myself crumbled.

The Earth Element of your foundation represents the necessity for food, water, and shelter. The Watery Element represents your imagination and desires, which change continually. The Fiery Element is that of control and passion, which creates our character and personality. The Airy Element represents acceptance and love, which resides in the heart. In the Bible it is said we are made of clay. If clay is molded and then put back into water it gradually melts back to a formless mud. If it is put into the Fiery Element and baked it holds that form. These hardened stories are what we have told ourselves many times and the desires we have pursued have forged our character and are more difficult to eliminate because they are like baked clay. To go back to the Bible, God breathed on the clay and it became human. So the Airy Element of breathing makes us alive and capable of acceptance and love. We come alive with our first breath and we die with our last breath.

Within yourself you have all the elements. Just as it takes time for water to soften earth and even eventually to break through rock, it will take time to attend to your emotions. Don't struggle to control. Be aware, be patient, have faith. As you go deeper, some artifacts may appear. Don't discount them, as they represent experiences from your past that you have forgotten about and you'll need to revisit them later.

When I got deeper into my unknown areas I realized how often I got hurt. Swami Radha one day asked me if I had many dreams. I told her I had a disturbing one about many children with bandages and blood and I felt helpless to help them. She thought for a minute and then said "Oh, do you often feel hurt?" I agreed, "Yes, I do". So she suggested that I put a Band-Aid on myself every time I felt hurt. After three days I had dozens of Band-Aids on myself. I realized how ridiculous this was and needed to explore why I was so sensitive. Of course it was my attachment to my ego that was being hurt.

As the well deepens you must be sure the wall of the well will not collapse. You need support. This is analogous to finding teachers, friends, fellow travelers and mentors; people who are interested in your journey, not those who make fun of it. Be wary of people who want to keep you in the same small box-- this often includes family and friends. Your daily discipline will begin to create change in your life. With years of devoted, disciplined practice you will reach water; a joyful life of honesty, trust, openness, respect and vulnerability.

The aim is to bring the sparkling clear water from the deep aspects of yourself to the surface, the conscious level. As unconscious human beings we are like muddy water; murky, stagnant, far from transparent, and frequently unclear. Just as it takes time for the well to be finished, it is only over time that the water always runs clear. When the good water is flowing, it is crystal clear and pure and can be used to enhance your daily life. Your discipline is the pump to bring the water to the surface of your consciousness. Without the pump the water gets stagnant; your daily practice is of prime importance. We would like to be always clear, authentic and radiant.

*"Believe in yourself, take on your challenges, dig deep within yourself to conquer fears. Never let anyone bring you down. You got to keep going."*
Chantal Sutherland

# Questions/Exercises:

1. What prod have you had from the universe to evolve?

2. What is the negative story you carry around in your head about yourself?

3. Rewrite your negative story with the plot, characters, and outcomes most pleasing to you.

# *Chapter 2*

# *The Garden*

*"Whether you tend a garden or not,*

*You are the gardener of your own being,*

*The seed of your destiny."*

Findhorn Community

The garden is a powerful metaphor for the journey to our authentic self. If you imagine yourself as a garden, would it be full of weeds and uncared for? Would it be barren, or flourishing and beautiful? Are there areas of yourself that are neglected where the weeds of thoughtlessness and unawareness have the potential to grow?

As a child I spent hours with my parents in their flower garden. They had busy lives so the time in the garden was precious; there was a deep sense of connection. Gardening was a joy, I didn't think about it. I effortlessly absorbed their love and knowledge for flowers. Following their pattern my interest for many years was in growing flowers.

Flowers have an amazing variety of shapes and colors that fascinate me. I think my love of color and variety comes from that admiration of nature's bounty, everything has a beauty of its own. But after living here in America I have also love growing vegetables and herbs that I can use in my cooking. Gardening has always been a source of delight when everything is going well and one of disappointment and learning when it is not.

Plants can keep you honest if you observe them and respond. Weeds are symbols of emotions that arise in certain situations as thoughtless negative reactions, something like jealousy or anger that keeps re-occurring in your life. They may arise out of guilt, out of actions you haven't taken or out of thanks that you haven't given. Take action. Just thinking about doing something, is not doing anything. Otherwise they will turn from beautiful flowers into the weeds of your mind again. Weeds are often old patterns learned when you were a child for your survival but no longer suitable in your life. Recall a basic survival instinct that you needed as a child but is now an inappropriate response. Become aware of what triggers that spontaneous outburst of emotion. Name it, then you can begin to become aware and live from choice and not reaction.

Weeds can overwhelm your garden, stopping it from being beautiful. They are not something you can ignore. You would like a weed-free garden but that's not achievable without constant attention. If the exact same weeds keep coming up – you find yourself in the same situation over and over again – find the source, the mother plant that is spreading the seeds, and dig it out. Going back to the root of the problem takes deep work, effort and commitment. This will solve the problem for some time but other weeds crop up and you need to continue to pay attention.

The quality of the soil is very important. Dig, loosen it up, and add compost or sand to make friable material for your plants to thrive. Compost is old vegetation that is going through transformation, returning to soil and making the earth richer. Without this process of renewal the soil is shallow or worse—it is dead lifeless dirt. This is analogous to you digging into yourself. This can reveal the "You" who exists beyond your daily busyness. Just as you turn the organic matter into the soil, so you sift and turn the layers of your own experience into knowledge and wisdom.

If you are to have a flourishing garden, you become aware of the natural elements—the sun, the rain, the shade, and the wind. Plants thrive in different regions and in different climates. What climate do you live in yourself? Are you an introvert or extrovert? Are you a people person or do you dislike exciting crowds and events? Are you generous, kind, compassionate and loving? What makes you comfortable and content?

Gardening forces you to be in the moment, to deal with what is here and now. For plants to grow they must have food, water, light and love just like you. If you see a plant drooping, water it. A well-tended garden can help you get over a tendency to procrastinate. Plants can't fake it like human beings.

Become aware of the natural elements in your life. The sun is analogous to the happy times, the rain may express the sad times from which we learn so much, while the wind could be those forces which seem to turn us to face a different direction. In a garden, be careful to put plants in the climate in which they most thrive, be it full sun or deep shade. Do you always feel you have to be sunny? Can you sometimes allow yourself to be in an inward and in a resting state like perennials that go dormant in the winter? Observe the elements of your life. Are they nurturing you or making you uncomfortable?

My husband and I were born in the same year. According to Chinese astrology, we were both Roosters. When we first married and I was involved with my children and at home I was like a Hen. When I evolved through yoga and started traveling, teaching workshops, I felt strong, wise, vigorous and content. Each time I returned home he felt he had to be the rooster and I should agree with everything he crowed. This made me feel schizophrenic. I felt like I was two different people. I'd go away and be one person and come back and needed to be entirely different; his "yes man." This became intolerable. I felt suffocated at home, a place where one should flourish. I was living in depleted soil. Not enough water and certainly missing the love of the sun. With a strong hope that the shallow soil of my marriage would change, I stuck it out while my boys grew up. After a very long ten years, in spite of tremendous guilt and pain, I uprooted myself and followed my dharma which was to devote myself to my practice and teaching. In twenty-twenty hindsight I can now see that it was a gift for both of us that I decided to leave so that we could each flourish on our separate paths.

There are two types of plants, Annuals and Perennials. You plant Annuals each year to provide joyful color and perfume to enhance your garden, like those temporary small pleasures you put into your life, going on a vacation or spoiling yourself in some way. To keep an annual garden beautiful you have to remove dead flowers throughout the growing season. The plant's biological pattern is to produce seeds. If you pay attention and prune the withering blooms off the plant it will often continue to produce, whereas when you leave the seeds the plants have satisfied their life cycle.

Perennials meanwhile are those plants, trees and shrubs that create the structure and design. These do not need replacing every year and may be moved to other locations. Of course you may wish to replace and redesign your garden as you change. Perennials need pruning back when they are growing woody. "Woody" is when large areas of a plant no longer produce leaves or flowers. At the simplest level pruning and training is to make sure perennials are as healthy and vigorous as possible. It requires the removal of dead, diseased or damaged parts. You might also want to prune to enhance the shape as in the science of topiary and bonsai. Sometimes it is the new growth that may need pruning to encourage the best results. Some plants, like roses, need to be pruned each year in the winter to encourage new growth and better blooms.

Sometimes it takes time in a garden to realize that there is an old perennial plant that you have loved— time to pull it out and replace it with a fresh start.

When I eventually decided to end my marriage it was like I was pulling out the roots of my relationship with my husband. He had been in my life since my I was 19. He had influenced me and helped me grow in many ways.

Getting free was a relief, but extremely painful and upsetting. I vacillated between feeling like I'd lost an arm and a leg, to feeling like a 15 year old, naïve in this new world. I realized I could do anything and I had a big decision to make, how was I going to live in the future? Would I replace him with a similar support, or would I be adventurous and find out what life on my own held. After a few years of emotional turmoil I felt totally free to follow my path.

I had gone to say with a friend in Idyllwild California and spent many days hiking in the San Bernardino Mountains. Seldom did I ever see another hiker; I felt I had the mountain to myself. One hot, sunny day, mid-week, while hiking I saw a massive rock, with a flat top; I climbed up, threw my clothes off and started dancing and chanting. The freedom was exhilarating. Two hikers walked by looking at this crazy old lady dancing on the rock. Undaunted I continued doing my thing! To this day I wonder what the story was that they told that night.

My marriage had lasted for 27 years and it was time for me to find out who I was without a partner. He was a perennial presence in my garden often choking out my own growth. My children had grown and left home and I could have shrunk into the shadow of my marriage or risk facing the sun on my own.

In your life, observe the people you live with or have as friends. Are they in harmony with the way you want to grow? Or are they people who are not interested in your new direction and would prefer that you stay the same? One way to look at personal change is to see yourself as a perennial. Are there dead, diseased or damaged areas in yourself, threatening your health and vigor?

The garden teaches us that it is process that creates the end result. You plant the seed, nurture it, continue to water and fertilize it paying attention so that it grows strong and beautiful. If you pay attention to the small things it makes life flow and you can experience life on a manageable scale. If you get over-enthused with a garden and try to reorganize too many aspects at one time, you will realize that one or two things are sufficient to pay attention to at one time. Basic needs come first. Look at your shelter. Is it pleasing to you? Do you eat food that is healthful and gives you energy? Do you wear clothes that enhance you and are comfortable?

While it is important to tend your garden, it is also important to relax within it and enjoy the quiet communion with nature, just like relaxing in the warmth of the sun on a lovely day, taking a walk amongst trees, or listening to bird calls and the small sounds of the wind in the leaves.

These small sounds are similar to the awareness that only speaks to us when we are quiet and not distracted by the outside world.

When I am feeling upset or overburdened in some way I find sitting in my garden and reading a book to distract myself from myself is the most creative thing I can do. Then my deeper mind can quiet down and often the idea of what I should do will rise up in my conscious mind.

*"Use the talents you possess, for the woods would be very silent if no birds sang except the best."*

Henry Van Dyke

Through bringing plants from seed to maturity we learn, step by step, the time it takes for growth to happen. Nothing in gardening teaches instant gratification. You need to be patient and persistent in your attention to bring change into fruition. The garden teaches you how to do your part by continued and unending attention and having patience for the seeds to germinate and sprout.

As you nurture these delicate plants and see that they get the right amount of attention they will grow stronger just as you pay attention to your daily life and nurture yourself you will have that similar pleasure in flourishing.

The decision to take on a practice is just the first step, like planting a seed. Your growth will be strengthened by awareness and continued practice. A garden is never done, never finished, there is no resolution. Change is the name of the game, as it is in your life. Remain fluid and accept the changes as you evolve and observe what is happening in your external world.

Plants were present in our world for millions of years before humanity and you can learn from them how to survive and be healthy. They have also adapted to us and learned to satisfy our needs and desires. If you ask indigenous people where they got their knowledge of the plants they will typically tell you that the information came from the plants themselves. We have lost the ability to communicate deeply with Mother Earth, but indigenous people's wisdom helps them to recognize earthly needs and values. So much of humanity has lost the ability to communicate on that deep level with nature. Even imagining digging the well into the earth connects us to our humanity on a very basic level. The water of the well sustains us.

"*We began as a mineral.*
*We emerged into plant life*
*And into animal state, and then into being human,*
*And always we have forgotten*
*Our former states, except in early spring when we*
*Slightly recall being green again.*"

Rumi

# *Questions/Exercises:*

1. What climate do you live in, what are your characteristics?

2. What are the annual areas of color and joy in your life?

3. If you've pruned some areas of your perennial life are they blooming again?

*When confronted with a challenge, the committed heart will search for a solution. The undecided heart searches for an escape.*

Andy Andrews

# *Chapter 3*

# *Commitment and Concentration*

*Until one is committed there is hesitancy*
*The chance to draw back, always ineffectiveness . . .*
*But the moment one definitely commits oneself, then Providence moves too.*
*All sorts of things occur to help one that would never otherwise have occurred.*
*A whole stream of events issues from the decision raising in one's favor.*
*All manner of unforeseen incidents and meetings and material assistance*
*which no man could have dreamt would have come his way.*
*Whatever you can do or dream you can begin it.*
*Boldness has genius, power and magic in it.*
*Begin it now.*

Attributed to Goethe

Commitment is probably the most difficult step in the progress of this journey, and the most important one. Without commitment to develop your awareness, things will develop very slowly. Continue to create the quiet times daily to develop your capacity for discernment.

Life is like a river, always moving. The views and banks are always changing. Make a commitment to give yourself daily time to be aware of the present and make your monkey mind quiet. You will make an anchor for yourself, a confidence that will be there for you under any circumstances. Trusting in yourself gives you inner strength and the stability to face anything.

In the beginning make your commitment a small one, perhaps fifteen minutes in duration. Promise yourself you will do it five days in the week at the same time, in the same place, as much as possible. You can always do it more if you like. After 21 days this habit, this support, can become an anchor in your life. Like brushing your teeth, you won't even need to think about it.

Remember you are committing yourself to your own inner growth. This is your unique direction, which may vary from others', even your teacher's. It takes courage to pursue commitment which includes ideas of dependability, resolution, respect and faithfulness.

Imagine you are an orangutan in the forest going through the forest swinging on vines, swinging from one to another. You come to a place where the next vine is far is beyond your reach. If you don't take the risk and allow yourself to have a short period with nothing to hold onto you will be stuck in place. It is often when you have the courage to let go of security for a moment that you can catch the next vine and complete your journey. If you hold onto security you will come to a standstill and have to drop to the floor of the forest.

Commitment helps you to deepen and explore that part of you that is in the shadows. Just as digging into the well reveals the deeper aspects, so does opening yourself up to new experiences. You may be afraid of the shadow because it is the unknown and may be negative. In this unexplored area there will be both negative and positive things that you will learn about yourself. The negative aspects may be unpleasant but they give you the opportunity of befriending that part of yourself, and in doing so become able to control it.

*"Keep knocking and the joy inside you will eventually open a window.*
*Look out and see who is there."*

Rumi

Changing the way you live your life is actually happening all the time on the external level. You change jobs, houses, relationships over and over again throughout your life. But this is the internal level-- considering changing your attitudes, the way you look at life. If you choose to evolve you must have courage to face the shadow side of yourself. It is a part of you and to become whole it is important to explore it.

The decision to focus requires commitment and interest, which is why your choice of practice is important. Remember it is your choice. You are your own authority. The practice should help you in your daily life to focus on what is present instead of what is in your mind. This helps to calm you and makes life more pleasant. You really have amazing powers of concentration available to you, but this depends on the urgency of the situation. When there is danger you are very alert and focused. By learning to focus your mind on awareness without drama or danger, you can have that same level of alertness and can understand yourself at a much deeper level.

Commitment to a practice helps you to get in touch with your destiny, which means your life is somewhat under your control. Fate, on the other hand takes place when there is an absence of purpose in the succession of events. The practice allows you to move onto a more flexible way of living the external life.

The way you live your life can be categorized because if it is something you know you feel secure to proceed. If it is something you don't know it brings fear and you often avoid it unless you are courageous and adventurous and accept the challenge. That is when you enter into the realm of yourself that you don't even know that you don't know, and you learn about yourself.

❖ **Blue** represents the things in life that you already know and you know that you know it, e.g. I know that I know how to walk.

❖ **Red** represents the things in life that you know that you don't know, e.g. I know that I don't know how to speak Chinese.

❖ Green represents all the things in life that are new, unknown, scary in the sense of not knowing how you will feel, be affected or react

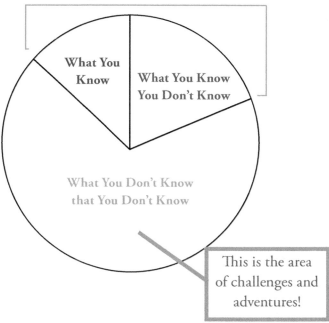

This is Living Within Your Survival Instincts?

What You Know

What You Know You Don't Know

What You Don't Know that You Don't Know

This is the area of challenges and adventures!

If you only live between the parameters of "what you know" and "what you know you don't know", you are living out of your survival instincts. You know the territory. Be courageous, discover your potential and move into the unknown. Yes, it may be scary and will not necessarily feel secure, but it is worth it. This unknown space is where we deepen the knowledge of ourselves.

Fear of revealing any apparently negative characteristic of yourself is the reason most people don't go on this adventure. The fear is like a monster that only grows bigger the more we run away but is actually a bully, and if you have the courage to turn and face it, to really look at it, then fear will shrink and diminish. And eventually even that so called negative aspect will become part of your knowledge about yourself and therefore under your control.

One day I set out with three other women on a ten day kayak trip in the Queen Charlotte Islands, beautiful Canadian islands north of Vancouver, still occupied by the Haida tribe. The outer islands have been declared a national park and are no longer inhabited. Before this trip I had only been kayaking for half an hour. The trip was to kayak from island to island, camping along the way. Unfortunately the weather was bad and it just rained and rained. About half way on our trip we became stuck on one island for four days and were anxious to get on our way. The weather signs morning and evening were not perfect. There were high little puffy clouds scudding across the sky. I didn't know anything about weather prediction, but my friend Kathryn who is an expert said we shouldn't go although it was sunny and felt calm, but she said the clouds meant there was a high wind coming. She said we had a four hour paddle with no place to shelter in. Still, after four days the sun was bright, all felt good enough to the rest of us. The puffy clouds were still moving fast high in the sky. Three of us decided we wanted to go. Kathryn did not agree. But we persisted and we all started off happily in the sun. In half an hour's time everything changed. First, big swells made us laugh as we paddled up the front and surfed down the back side. Then the reality of our situation hit us as we looked behind to see huge black clouds reaching for us and the race to get off the water began. Even in calm waters, we had a four hour paddle to land. The storm wrapped itself around us and playful swells became terrifying monsters driven by vicious winds. I had borrowed a kayak that had a very long nose, not realizing that the long nose made me vulnerable to the wind. Not being a knowledgeable kayaker I was rapidly becoming aware of my desperate situation. The wind played with my stupidity and would catch that ridiculously long nose like a horizontal sail and spin me again and again out toward the open ocean. Each time the wind caught me, my skilled kayaking friend saved me by staying close and repeatedly hitting the back of my kayak with her hand, keeping me on course.

About two hours into the high seas, with each stroke of my paddle, I chanted vehemently: "Om Namah Shivya, Om Namah Shivya, Om Namah Shivya", which was a plea to take this storm away. The chanting which was a familiar and well-rehearsed practice helped to stop my mind from going into hysterical panic at the scary life threatening situation we found ourselves in. My mind kept saying "I can't do it, I won't make it, I can't paddle another stroke." I linked my chanting to my paddling so I could keep going. At long last we came into a bay, and landed on a sandy beach. Ah, the safety of ground under my feet. This was a challenge my rational mind thought I could not survive and yet my deeper desire for more life and my practices overcame that outcome.

Quantum physics supports the phenomenon of total commitment as being something that pulses and changes the outcome. Don't listen to your doubts which tell you that you are small and ordinary, you are a unique expression of a human being and as such are a precious piece of the whole Universe.

Our world has become so fast our level of concentration has gone down. Often we are unable to separate from our screens and endless images being shot at us at an enormous rate. Everything has speeded up, even speech, and we are said to have an attention span of less than two minutes. Practice is to give you the gift of a space each day to be quiet and inwardly centered, a time to quiet the chatter of your monkey mind. It is called "monkey mind" because it is continually chattering away in your head.

The first step in learning to concentrate is to be in the present. Don't be attached to what is in your mind. The mind is like an elephant's trunk, never still. A good "mahout" gives his elephant a stick to carry in his trunk if they are going to go through a village street. If the elephant doesn't have this task it will create mayhem by grabbing a banana here, an umbrella there, leaving the village in an uproar.

To practice concentration is important as otherwise you add another story about yourself. "I can't concentrate." The words you tell yourself are important.

❖ *Did – is a word of achievement*

❖ *Won't – is a word of retreat*

❖ *Might – is a word of bereavement*

❖ *Can't – is a word of defeat*

❖ *Ought – is a word of duty*

❖ *Try – is a word each hour*

❖ *Will – is a word of beauty*

❖ *Can – is a word of power*

Gerard Hargarves

*Exercise:* **Using the breath to quiet your mind:**

Start keeping track of your natural breath, then close your eyes and see the numbers 1 to 9 light up as you inhale. Do this repeatedly for five minutes. If your mind gets caught by a thought or you lose track, just start again at 1. Be patient with yourself. In the beginning it is difficult to keep the mind on track.

Then change your attention to your exhalation, again seeing the numbers 1 to 9 light up in your mind's eye as your exhale. If you lose track or get sleepy, start again at 1. Practice for five minutes being patient with yourself.

After practicing this way for about a week you will have information about your mind. Inhalation is the phase when the mind naturally gets busy. We call breathing "inspiration", a word that also means "to get ideas". This is because the brain and the nervous system are connected.

Exhalation is the relaxing phrase of the brain and can lead to drifting away.

Both in and out breaths should be through the nose. The East Indians say, "You don't try to eat with your nose, why do you try to breathe with your mouth?"

During which phrase does your mind get distracted, either with extraneous thoughts or finding yourself getting sleepy? Observe when your mind loses track of the repetitive numbers as each one lights up. Do you need to calm your mind or liven it up? When your mind becomes evenly focused you will become inwardly attentive.

This practice may take time to master and needs patience and a positive attitude. Saying "I can't do it" will get you nowhere. It takes commitment.

As you change your attitudes and interests you may have to change your relationships and friends. New relationships and friends that support your new direction in life are important. Otherwise you feel isolated and give up.

As my practice became established I did it after my husband and children had left for work and school. I didn't do the usual housewife tasks of cleaning up, making beds and going shopping. I put my practice first and tackled those things afterwards. Doing my practice first in the morning has continued since 1963. Practice time is practice time. Train yourself to be focused and ignore all other diversions.

I was in North Carolina, teaching the Friday night class of a weekend workshop. I saw a student who needed an adjustment and moved quickly towards them. I stepped on a book and whoosh, down I went onto my right hand. The moment I went down I knew I had broken my wrist. After the hospital visit I was determined to fulfill my commitment. With the help of an experienced student as my assistant, I taught the rest of that weekend seminar with a huge cast on my arm, though I did cancel my next workshop.

Seven weeks after my cast was removed, I went to India to do an Invitational Back Bend Workshop. Before going, while still in a cast, I had stayed true to my daily practice. Standing poses were no problem, sitting poses were no problem, figuring out how to do headstands and a shoulder stand with a cast was an adventure into the unknown, but I found a way.

I was not able to practice back bends because that requires directly pressing my full body weight up from the floor with my arms over my head. During the workshop I was challenged to start doing backbends even though the scar tissue left from the injury caused tremendous pain. The courage came from my faith in my teacher and my commitment. Doing backbends broke the scar tissue free and gave me back full range of movement in my wrist which was something else the doctors had said I would never have.

Commit yourself to accepting and meeting challenges that life presents you with. They are the ways life helps us to evolve. Some may create disappointment at first, but in 20/20 hindsight you will be able to see the gifts of wisdom and knowledge you have gained about yourself.

Many years ago there was a book that postulated that there were many levels of human development and that the majority of people are not very interested in exploring their inner selves. They are happy living with "what they know" and "what they know they don't know", in other words they are happy living within their survival instincts. The book explained it this way:

> *"There are human beings that are so dense that they have little life-- Mineral Man. People who are dense as a rock. Then there are juicier ones; Vegetable Man Then we come to Animal Man—happy if they have shelter, food, clothes, sex & fun. Man Man is where there is awareness, curiosity, and courage to pursue a full life. Then there is God Man, there is no such human being that is totally this."*

M.B. Chanda

If we are committed and curious, and making progress, we are a mixture of Man Man and God Man.

*"Perseverance is a great element of success.
If you only knock long enough and loud enough at the gate,
You are sure to wake up something, or somebody."*

Henry Wadsworth Longfellow

## *Question / Exercise*

In closing this chapter I invite you to take time and personalize the quote at the beginning of this chapter. I have found it to be very inspiring, especially during times of uncertainty or when I want to take a leap that frightens me. To this day, I have posted my personalized version on my refrigerator.

Until I *am* committed there is hesitancy
the chance to draw back, always ineffectiveness
But the moment *I* definitely commit *myself,* then Providence moves too.
All sorts of things occur to help me. . . .

# Chapter 4

# *Communication*

*"A life unexamined is a life not worth living."*
Voltaire

Making serious changes demands close attention to your outward life. Look for actions or words that create suffering or discontent in you or others. Begin to develop a sense of detachment from your ego so that you can be honest with yourself about your strengths and weaknesses. Where do your negative thoughts come from? What is their basis? Is it fear, anger or frustration, or is it letting the imagination run wild? If you can identify the emotion that is driving you, then you can develop control. Personal problems often take root in thoughts and emotions that are negative and are making your life uncomfortable. These are like the weeds in the garden. They don't make your life beautiful. Don't bother wasting time and energy imagining potential negative outcomes, rather, use your imagination to create a wonderful life.

Actions are the result of old patterns or of unconscious thoughts and can reveal yourself to yourself as you become aware of them. You are often acting from reflex, not truly paying attention but repeating old patterns. If you have chosen your direction you can observe what is taking you in that direction and which actions and words are not. These are what you want to become aware of in the present.

As Portia Nelson says in her famous poem,
"Autobiography in Five short Chapters"
a bad habit is like a hole in the ground.

We frequently fall into our bad habit
and think it isn't our fault.
We flail around blaming everyone
and denying that we had anything
to do with this difficulty.
But still, there we are back
in the same hole again.
And this keeps us stuck.
Living life without recognition
of personal responsibility
leads to an endless
loop of struggle.

The sooner we become more aware
and realize that it is our fault,
then we are able to change
our behavior and eventually
make new choices.

Only then can we walk down
a new path.

Communication goes through three stages. First we think, but thoughts are very evanescent, we can forget what we thought a minute ago, it changes very quickly.

The next stage is to verbalize that thought; this manifests it to a certain extent by affecting the airwaves. Unless there is a recorder present, this also disappears very fast. How often has someone said to you, "But you said." and you say, "No, I never did say that." There is no longer any proof either way.

*Inaudible Speech:*  Become aware of how much you talk to yourself. However, when you write something down you really have brought that thought into manifestation. It is there in black and white and you cannot deny that thought or the recognition of that feeling at that time.

There is a practice from Swami Radha, called the "Spiritual Diary". It is a way to develop control of your weeds—the things that make you fall into the same hole again and again.

## *Spiritual Diary: A Practice to Become Aware of Habits*

- ❖ First make a list from your life of the things that create problems or suffering for yourself or others.

- ❖ Next, choose the two actions that create the most problems for you. These two are the actions or words that you want to control at first.

- ❖ Bring them into your awareness by writing in your Spiritual Diary every 24 hours. Briefly relive those 24 hours and remember if those actions or words came up. If so, what was the situation?

- ❖ Write whether you were even aware of it at that time and what your reaction was. Remember that this should be done every day.

- ❖ The journaling is just to note the incident and your reaction, not to blame or congratulate yourself. Usually, doing this repeatedly, your awareness of your button being pushed comes closer and closer to your consciousness, and then one day, in the present, you catch yourself reacting in the same old way and you decide to react differently.

- ❖ This is just the beginning. You will have more unconscious reactions to work on, but only be checking on two at a time until you are able to choose how to act in those situations.

- ❖ By writing and reading your Spiritual Diary you are clarifying yourself to yourself, in black and white, a manifestation that cannot be denied.

You are now seeing that the difference between thought—ideas we create in our head—and what is actually going on are two different things. Without checking your thoughts with the reality around you are living a life of delusion. This exercise I did at the ashram made me aware of how often I was living in delusion.

When I was at the Ashram we were instructed to do a practice for a week that was challenging to us. The practice I chose was to ask people if my remarks that I believed were hurtful, had in fact been hurtful to them. Most of the time people didn't even remember the incident. S o thinking I'd hurt someone without checking it out, I had responded to them believing they were hurt or angry with me. This created a false relationship where I was relating to my belief and not to reality. So, as soon as I was aware of my uncomfortable feelings I then checked their reaction. My practice was to ask them what they were feeling, and they often did not even remember my remark. Doing this allowed me to relate to the person rather than relating to my internal made up thoughts which made me apologetic, timid and reluctant to face them—altering our friendship. I realized I was living a life of delusion.

Two truths here: one, that reality is not what we think, our thinking is always only an interpretation. And two, what we think in reaction to some experiences is what creates our suffering. If you don't check it out, and the other person does not even know you are upset then you are creating suffering for yourself. When someone says something that you believe was meant to hurt you, you are able to ask them if that was their intent?

You must realize that you are totally responsible for your choices: You are the one making the choice and are responsible for these thoughts, words and actions. No excuses.

Why is it so common to doubt yourself? Is it because you identify with the ego aspect of yourself as if it is real and as if that is all that you are. To progress, replace the negative stories with positive ones. Be patient and diligent, understand that this work on yourself takes time, energy and awareness, and will not produce results overnight. It is a long continuous commitment to your growth and contentment. Remember that in the garden there are many weeds, and they continue to grow and require continual time and attention. Plucking a single weed will not give you the garden you desire.

*"If you are vigilant*
*You can*
*Change each circumstance of your life*
*Each action*
*Each movement an occasion*
*For coming nearer the goal."*

The Mother

Communication with your body is also wise. The body communicates to you through feeling, which is quite different than thinking. Feeling is a message, a sensation that comes from your body. Your body is very wise and you can trust it. The body is the most external of your manifestations and it is important to keep it in good health. When you are not feeling well it is difficult to concentrate your mind on other aspects. There are ethics for the treatment of this house of yours: exercise regularly, eat wisely, get enough sleep and be in touch with it so you can notice more and more subtle messages. Discomfort in your body means it is asking for attention, and by attending to it, you learn when something is not quite right and are able to take action. Take responsibility and first decide what you can do about the problem. Sometimes it takes simple action, other times you may need some help.

For many years I ignored clear messages from my body. I went for the quick fix until my body screamed "No more!" Following is one of my examples of waiting too long to ask for help.

When I was 18, at university, I was on the swimming team. I was the "Backstroker" and at that time you had to hit the wall of the swimming pool with your hand before you "tumble turned". In doing this I dislocated my left shoulder. Life had already conditioned me to downplay all moments of personal need. So, I simply popped my shoulder back into place by myself. Yes it hurt! But it fit with my inner message of "don't make a fuss." Several years later I fell downstairs and dislocated that same shoulder again. From then on, my shoulder would dislocate very easily. Each time, with no fuss, but great pain, I relocated it myself. The time came when my relocating it no longer worked and I had to go to an emergency room. It was time to do something more. By then I had a three and a half year old son, an eighteen month old son, and was five months pregnant. It was not a good time to have an operation, but it needed to be done. I had a four hour operation, and my arm was bound to my side for six weeks. The prognosis was not good. The doctor said, "If you ever dislocate your shoulder again, God help you because no man will be able to help you." He told me I would never lift that arm above the shoulder again and would not be able to put my left hand behind my head. Those six weeks were some of the most difficult times in my life to live through.

Your thoughts are private but they are revealed in your speech and actions. Your thoughts are the deepest layer of your conscious mind, and, like the weeds in the garden, you must pay attention as you become aware of them. Your thoughts are inaudible speech, the way you communicate with yourself. Thoughts come and go at a dizzying speed, they are hard to hang on to, and you are very good at pretending you don't have negative thoughts. Taking time to be quiet and reflective, being open to the present with yourself, and writing down what you remember thinking will help you to clarify yourself.

*Quiet the mind, and the soul will speak.*
Ma Jaya Sati Bhagavati

*Exercise: "Straight Line Thinking" a practice to look at both sides.*

***I have used this exercise that I learned from Swami Radha, many times when I'm not sure which way to go.***

❖ First, pose a question to yourself. (e.g. I need to move to Seattle.)

❖ Take the opposite position. (e.g. I don't need to move to Seattle)

❖ Make a list of the advantages of this and another list of the disadvantages

❖ Now put the same question in the negative and make a list of advantages and disadvantages from that point of view. For example after making positive and negative lists for "I want to move to Seattle", you would make lists for "I don't want to move to Seattle." Switching the question from positive to negative provokes different thinking; drawing from different parts of your brain.

❖ Wait a few days, be patient, let the decision sit in your soul. Wait until your subconscious has time to consider it. The longest list is not necessarily the answer. Then the correct answer will come into your conscious mind and your gut "belly brain" will feel comfortable.

Neuroscience has documented that the human body has three brains. One in your head, one in your gut and one in your heart. Your heart and your subconscious are connected with the decision if you give it time. This is why it is a truth that you deal more affectively with critical questions after you've "slept on it".

Patience is part of the process of making decisions, planting the seed and waiting for it to sprout, allowing time to think and look more deeply. It is the positive side of waiting. Impatience is acting too quickly without thought. Procrastination is delaying action on something you already know you need or want to do. Allowing your subconscious to have its say is wise. Until you are adept in knowing yourself, learn not to say "Yes" to every request, but learn to say, "I will think about it" giving the subconscious time to have its say. It is often wiser than your rational mind. When the subconscious speaks and the answer is "no," honoring it is the next step toward being authentic. You don't need to do everything you are asked to do. Learn to be discerning and honest. Patience gives you time to tune in and know what is true for you.

*Audible Speech:*     With audible speech, you are expressing (expressing means to squeeze out) your thoughts and bringing them into a form of manifestation, affecting the airwaves. They are quick to disappear unless you have recorded them. Emotions often reveal themselves in audible speech, because the voice is the vehicle of emotions. With a friend, if one word is spoken you can often tell that they are having problems because the tone of the voice is stressed, the voice reveling the emotions. Listen carefully to your own words and tone as this will help you to tune into yourself.

It is important to look closely at your emotional responses. Righteous anger has tremendous value, and is a response in the moment, a truthful expression of feeling. Unrighteous anger is when you've tucked it away and it sours and creates unconscious emotions. If you hang on to anger or fear, they become your internal boundaries, inside of which you build your life. If on the other hand, you hang on to love and compassion, your world and life will reflect that love.

At the ashram during the three month course of development, one of the practices was to write about one of my negative emotions. This I did privately, it was my homework. Next day at the group I read my writings, and although I had written with no emotions coming up, as soon as I started reading I began to cry. As the voice is the vehicle for emotions, this happened to many people in the group.

I chose to work on anger. From that exercise I realized that my anger was nearly always attached to the feeling that I was disappointed because I had built up expectations. I would build castles of unspoken hopes that were not fulfilled, creating an internal anger that I was holding on to. Putting the blame onto them. This is irresponsible and unrighteous anger! It is not fair to be angry, I would even say it is stupid, to be angry with someone who doesn't meet an unexpressed expectation. I realized that they didn't know I was angry and that this was a very destructive thing that I was doing to myself. My learning was to be honest and when I had expectations to express them. But it also meant I tried to be more aware of my tendency to build unspoken hopes in my mind. From this lesson I experienced life with a new level of clarity.

Without this self-awareness I would have l continued to live a life of underlying anger and disappointment. This exercise was a way to clear out my negative emotions and has allowed me to be and live a much more loving and peaceful life.

❖ Is your voice soft for fear of saying something wrong or is it that you don't really want to be heard?

❖ Is your voice strong and powerful because there is a determination to be heard or to override others?

❖ Is it strong and clear because your mind is clear?

❖ Are you uncomfortable with silence and then do you chatter about inconsequential things?

Energy is wasted in useless chatter. Talking takes energy and you realize this when you've been very ill and you've had a visitor who wants you to talk.

Words are symbols, and for each person have different meanings and associations. Communication by words alone, for example email, is suspect and often misinterpreted. There are words which obviously carry emotional content, but even a word like "dog" brings up different feelings, pictures and reactions. If you can see the person and use the clues of facial expression or body language, you have a better chance at clear communication. In the modern technical world you are relying more and more just upon words and you as the writer are responsible for communicating the expression. Refining your language is important. Many words are somewhat similar but carry different overtones, for example, judgement/discernment, thrifty/stingy, fate/destiny, grab/reach for, benevolence/kindness, relaxed/lazy, kind/compassionate, content/complacent.

*Writing:*     In communicating through writing, you are manifesting your thoughts in black and white, an indisputable record, not to be denied. To become aware of your thoughts is the most important aspect of this journey and is the root of your speech and actions. Writing to yourself about your feelings is one of the best ways of clarifying your motives.

Writing in my diary and being true to myself enabled me to deal with the situation where my husband became a cross-dresser and chose to go public. This was a very embarrassing situation for me, but I tolerated it for ten years because I believed he would change. I didn't want to break the family up while the children were small. Looking back on it I can see that my decision to stay with him for so long made me strong. It was because I was true to myself in my diary that I was clear what my motives were for staying. Eventually, when the boys were grown, it was time to stop my sacrifice and continue on my own path. So at 52 I divorced my husband of 25 years and became single again. Quite a challenge as we had met when we were only 18 and for 25 years had lived my husband's life as was the general situation for women at that time. My passion developed when I realized I had more potential than wife and mother and I now stood on the edge of living my own life.

*"The breeze of dawn has secrets to tell you. Don't go back to sleep!*
*You must ask for what you really want. Don't go back to sleep!*
*People are going back and forth across the doorsill where the two worlds touch.*
*The door is round and open. Don't go back to sleep!"*

Rumi

*Dreams:*  Dreams are the deepest form of communication you have with your creative unconscious. Your subconscious uses symbols from your daily life to help you understand yourself better. Though not all dreams are significant, if they come into your conscious mind as you wake up, pay attention to them.

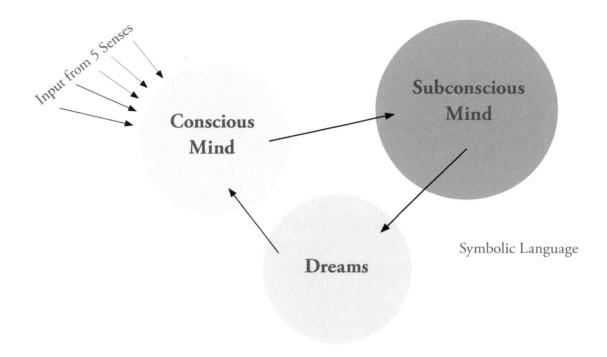

It is tempting to ask an expert to help you, but you are the only one who can discern the meaning of symbols appearing in your dream. The associations that you have with the nouns (person, place, thing) are uniquely yours. You will need to learn how to interpret them. Below is one method where you make associations with nouns.

## *Exercise:* for Interpreting Dreams

❖ Remember the nouns (person, place, thing) in the dream are symbols that occur in your daily life. If the nouns are people it is what they represent to you.

❖ Make a list of the nouns

❖ Forget the dream and write your four or five associations you have with the nouns

❖ From these associations pick one intuitively that jumps out at you

❖ Understand that the dream is about you, everything in the dream, every noun in the dream is representative of an aspect of yourself.

❖ After you have completed the list of associations, read the dream again substituting the associative word and adding "part of me". This will usually give you a good idea of the dream's message.

### *Example:*

I dreamt of food. My associations were nurturance, sustenance, fulfillment, love, and kitchen. I chose the association of fulfillment. I understood that I was dreaming of the fulfillment part of me.

❖ Do this for every noun and then put them back into your dream remembering to say "part of me" after the chosen substitute.

### *Another Example:*

When I was at the Yasodhara Ashram I had a dream where Mary was a peer who had had a similar life to mine. I dreamt that Mary and I were flying high in the sky enjoying looking down on the earth. Suddenly, I felt myself going into a downward dive and thought I was going to crash into the earth. Mary caught me by the back of my neck and the seat of my pants and we both zoomed up again into the area of safety.

❖ Mary – Divine Mother

❖ Peer – an earthly equal

❖ Sky – openness

❖ Earth – stable

- ❖ Neck – delicate part of me
- ❖ Seat – stability
- ❖ Pants – reaction to fear (NOTE: Pants is a symbol, but allow yourself the freedom to look at other meanings to a word. In this example the "pants" you wear could also be the "panting" shallow breath we often use out of fear.

The interpretation would replace the nouns with your association to the noun. It would sound like this: I had a dream where Mary (the divine part of myself) was a peer (my earthly equal) who had had a similar life to mine. I dreamt that Mary (the divine part of myself) and I (the earthly part of myself) were flying high in the sky (in the openness part of myself) enjoying looking down on the earth (the earthly part of myself). Suddenly, I felt myself going into a downward dive and thought I was going to crash. Mary (the divine part of myself) caught me by the back of my neck (a delicate part of myself) and the seat (the stable part of myself) of my pants and we both zoomed up again into the area of safety.

I interpreted this dream, as Mary represented the Divine Mother part of myself and would always save me if I was in danger of getting caught in my earthly problems. My earthly problem at that time was my divorce. It was a dream of faith in the guiding part of me.

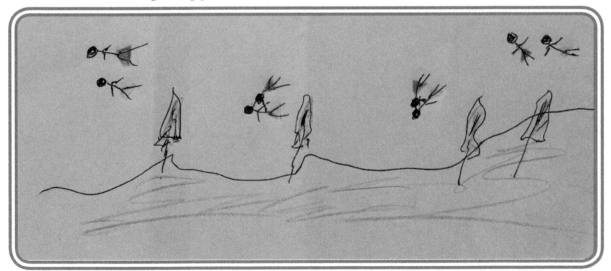

This was the way I remembered the dream. Stick figures are fine — you don't have to be an artist.

While still living at the Yashodara Ashram I had another vivid dream.

I was in a forest and noticed many rocks tumbled around. I realized that this had once been a floor and started to replace them. I then realized that it had been a circular floor, I couldn't find the rocks to complete it; they were missing.

I understood this to mean I still had work to do to complete my foundation.

Trust dreams like these that are so vivid when you wake up. Write the dream down as soon as possible, before your monkey mind has time to change it. Some dreams are very simple and direct while others take a while to work out.

Had the feeling not been so strong, my most direct and eventually most important dream was in fact so brief I could have easily dismissed it. The dream was just the words "You are living on Lopez Island" and I awoke felt ecstatically happy, whole and content, and filled with joy. I thought Lopez Island was a dream place, not a real location. The memory of this amazing feeling called me to keep the possibility alive that one day I might experience this unbelievable delight.

After leaving the ashram I moved to Seattle. A couple of years later, I saw an advertisement for property on Lopez Island and instantly remembered the dream. Asking around, I found it is the name of an island in the San Juans which I had also had never heard of. They turned out to be a group of islands off the coast north of Seattle. I found out how to get there I had to catch a ferry and on the trip over I began to have doubts of what I was going to learn by driving around an island? An idea popped into my head, "Pretend you want to buy a property." I looked in the local paper that was onboard, and upon arriving, phoned a realtor. He offered to drive me to see three inexpensive properties. Two were just a piece of forested land while the third had a small one room cabin on it with a deck that was falling off. The realtor showed me a lovely cedar grove on the left hand side. We walked into the grove, a beautiful circular space surrounded by old cedar trees, and immediately my inner being was excited, but, I was being sensible. I thanked him and then left. My real motive in seeing him was to question him about the island; population, doctor, lawyer, etc. I really had no intention to buy a property.

I left and for a month I found I could not forget about the cedar grove. The feeling was with me day and night. I recognized that I must follow up on this message that just wouldn't let me go.

I decided to go back and look at other places, thinking I would realize how silly I was being. I felt it was ridiculous with my financial state to consider buying property. I continued to tell myself I had no intention of buying property. I was just going back to dispel my attraction to this one piece of property. After seeing several others that had no appeal I asked to go back to the cedar grove. As we walked into the property we were surprised

to see the deck had been replaced. The caretaker for the property did not know it was on the market and had replaced the deck. When I walked into the cedar grove it had the same magical effect upon my being.

I knew this meant something important. I said, "Tell me about this property." At that time property on Lopez was at an all-time low. The owner would carry the loan and he wanted 10% as a down payment. I was a single woman with no credit history, my husband had gotten the benefit of all our credit history. What could I to do?

Upon arriving home I phoned an insurance company that I had invested in. I asked, "How much can I borrow?" Their answer, exactly the amount of the down payment! This was beyond exciting, an improbable gift, although I was still not sure that I would earn enough to pay the mortgage and would have to draw money from my small savings. I consulted a trusted friend for advice, and decided to "let go of the vine" I would take the leap and buy the property.

I felt that providence had played its part and I had the responsibility to play mine. I pondered why all these apparently serendipitous events had meant that I, with no credit, had been able to buy this exquisite property. I made it my mission to honor this gift from the universe by creating a Summer Yoga Retreat where students from the city could come for an intensive week of yoga while enjoying this beautiful, nurturing, rustic surrounding.

This property was 10 acres, with some lovely old trees, including a massive 300 year old Douglas Fir. I called this the Shiva Tree and used its symbolism with the students who came for retreats. Shiva is the East Indian quality of letting go. This tree had many, many holes from woodpeckers and I encouraged students to write briefly what they wanted to let go of and put their note in one of the holes. At the end of the week they took them out of the tree and brought them to our fire to burn them in a symbolic act of freeing themselves from what they felt was a limiting way of being.

I named the property Lavanya—*naturally beautiful*—a word from Sanskrit which is the ancient language of India. The first three years I offered my Seattle students yoga in trade for weekend work of helping to prepare the property. It was a wonderful way to create the retreat center as there were many ideas and lots of input. During this time I continued to live in Seattle while the property development continued. I built a lovely Yoga Pavilion and for twelve years, every summer, held several week long retreats for students.

The result of this lovely story is that my income increased to match the mortgage payment and I never did have to draw money to cover it.

In 1997 I moved to Lopez and rented a house for three years and continued the retreats until I sold Lavanya in order to build a house. I have lived on Lopez Island ever since, a wonderful community of people with very forward looking ideas, and a beautiful place surrounded by ocean and distant mountains.

How happy I am that I had the courage to take that leap of faith and follow my inner knowing rather than my rational intelligence.

*"May the stars light your way and may you find
the interior road forward".*

*Traditional Irish Farewell*

## Questions/Exercises:

1. Have you ever not taken a chance and regretted it afterwards?

2. Were your parents adventuresome or were they conservative?

3. Are your communications usually clear? In which aspect do you realize that you have an internal editor?

*It is better to conquer yourself*

*than to*

*win a thousand battles.*

*Then the victory is yours.*

*It cannot be taken from you,*

*not by angels or by demons,*

*heaven or hell.*

*Buddha*

# Chapter 5

# *Discipline and Practice*

*"Our deepest fear is not that we are inadequate.*
*Our deepest fear is that we are powerful beyond measure.*
*It is our light, not our darkness that most frightens us.*
*We ask ourselves, who am I to be brilliant, gorgeous, talented and fabulous?*
*Actually, who are you not to be?*
*You are a child of God. You playing small doesn't serve the world.*
*There's nothing enlightened about shrinking, so that other people*
*won't feel insecure around you.*
*We are born to make manifest the glory of God that is within us.*
*It's not just in some of us; it's in everyone.*
*And as we let our own light shine, we unconsciously give*
*other people permission to do the same.*
*As we are liberated from our own fear, our presence automatically liberates others."*

*Inaugural speech by* Marianne Williamson

If you take the quote above and personalize it, what messages does it give you? For example; "It is my light, not my darkness that most frightens me." What does this provoke in you? What memories, relationships, opportunities come to mind where you have shrunk from your own light? Continue on with each line.

It would read like this:

> My, deepest fear is not that I am inadequate.
> My, deepest fear is that I am powerful beyond measure.

Do you have the courage it takes to step out of normal patterns? Don't listen to your usual doubts, which tell you that you are small and ordinary. You are a unique expression of a human being and as such are precious when you express your talents to create Light in the world. Think of how every little spark of a flame makes it brighter. This is what your life could be about, rising to your potential as a happy, loving, and responsible human being.

Discipline is a word you have to think about. As a child it often had a negative connotation, being disciplined by somebody, either harshly or kindly. The discipline that you are choosing should have no harshness or negative results. You decide for yourself what your discipline will be. To become experienced and skilled in anything you must practice every day. Musicians and athletes understand this necessity and practice every day to nurture these new habits. You choose to discipline yourself and the discipline of that habit takes you in the direction of expanding yourself to live your life creatively. To know yourself and be authentic you are willing to explore those aspects that are beyond your survival instincts. We are not all the same. Here are two opposing ways of being:

One type of person would say, I'm a rather unstructured person. I like spontaneity and don't yearn for a routine. I like meeting new people, trying new foods, and going to new places. If I don't have some structure in my practice it can become too random. Life produces many choices, and being open to all these choices as I am, I need some consistency to go deeply into things or I am always on the surface. People like me need to impose some routine upon themselves.

Or, the other type would be people who tend to thrive on a routine. Those people have to be sure that they're not just sucked into the routine itself. They need to ensure there is room for some spontaneity. The routine can be very complex, but they have to be conscious they are not practicing in a thoughtless, robotic manner.

Developing self-discipline and practice that lead to your growing in happiness are the most important things.

*"Beyond real freedom, there lies real discipline."*
Erwin Mcanus

Practice time is practice time. The easiest way to introduce a new practice into your life is to do it at the same time and in the same place every day. Train yourself to be focused and ignore all other diversions except emergencies. Hold your practice time as sacred but not rigid. Promise yourself you will practice five days a week. You can always do seven, but this gives you that space, if necessary, to goof off. Of course illness and other unforeseen events can sometimes disturb this rhythm.

*"Put it at the top of your list."*
B.K.S. Iyengar

In society people tend to live a life that is externally oriented. They live from event to event and forget about the vertical aspect of themselves. This world is very hypnotic and demanding. If you want to evolve it is important to explore the heights and depths of yourself. You can't explore deeply going from event to event. To experience other dimensions of yourself it is imperative that you create space and time for your practice.

*"You are the World."*
Krishnamurti

Transformation starts with changing the small habitual ways of responding to life. Some habits and pleasures are appropriate at certain times of life, others may need to be modified, and still others may meaningfully stay with you all your life. Remember this is all a matter of your choosing. You are totally responsible for your life and how you choose to live it. Some habits are often repeated and become automatic and it takes awareness to observe them. Some of your habits are self-destructive, for instance going for immediate pleasure even though you know the result will not be a good outcome. If, in contrast, you choose something less alluring that you know will have a good outcome, then you are practicing discipline.

*"If you look after the root of the tree, the fragrance and flowering*
*of the tree will come of itself."*

B.K.S. Iyengar

Sometimes the change is made for you and you either resist it or are willing to adjust. Challenges are the way life presents you with these opportunities to transform yourself. Accept the challenge and move into this new area of experience.

One problem with discipline and practice is that in the beginning you may become over-enthusiastic. Remember that if a fire burns too hot all the fuel burns away quickly. A small but sincere commitment at first, maybe 15 minutes, will help you to establish this new habit. You can slowly extend the time and energy you devote to it as you recognize the benefits. Practice should have a positive effect on your daily life, a feeling of being more centered and able to deal with events.

Practice comes from the root "to do, to take action". It is a practical decision you are making to enhance your awareness and connection to the deeper aspects of yourself.

Real growth has unpredictability. The old feels comfortable and most everyone is afraid of change because it takes you into the realm of the unknown. However when life is prodding you because of physical or psychological discomfort, accept the challenge and begin exploring. Challenges, and accepting them, are the ways life offers to help us evolve. Even if you "fail" you learn something else about yourself. It may initially create disappointment within yourself, but in hindsight you will be able to see the wisdom you've gained and celebrate what you've learned.

Your practice may change as you proceed: use your inner intelligence to recognize and respond to the need for adjustment.

I found for myself it is best to do my practice first thing in the morning. This sets my day up, and gives me a center which supports me throughout my day. But this is my way, and each one of you has to find their own rhythm, the right practice and time, and pursue it with commitment and gratitude. As you continue you will come to a deeper understanding of yourself… a unique manifestation of the Spirit. This center which is like the flowing waters will slowly become more and more your way of being.

Experience is the only way to KNOW something; otherwise it is just an intellectual idea. It takes courage and time to believe in your own inner wisdom. To practice is to experience your authentic self, not the external cardboard figure society develops. A teacher gives you the tools, then it is your responsibility to use them every day.

There will be occasions when it is time to take a diversion or a break. Like the annuals that you add to the garden, you sometimes need something to add color and perfume to your garden. There is nothing wrong with pleasure. But with time, your choices for diversion might ideally become events that take you in your direction rather than serving as instant gratification.

At other times you may feel stuck and dry. Look for inspiration, attend a workshop, read another book and see what ideas come to you. Keep checking with your Spiritual Diary to see that you are remembering your new enlightenments. Maybe it is the practice that has become too familiar and automatic and needs to be more challenging, or the discipline to do the practice is lacking. If this is the case begin your practice again.

*"By practicing regularly you can break through the bonds that hold you.*
*On this path effort never goes to waste and there is no failure."*
Bhagavad Gita 2:39:40

If your discipline has become disturbed or lost because of illness or a protracted trip, be a saint and start again. An everyday saint is someone who falls down and then gets up and goes on. Remember it is always your responsibility and choice. What you do is more important than what you think.

*"Look to this day for it is Life,*

*The very Life of Life.*

*In its brief course lie all the realities and truths of existence.*

*The joy of growth,*

*The splendor of action,*

*The glory of power;*

*For yesterday is but a memory*

*And tomorrow is only a vision.*
*Look well therefore to this day."*

*Old Sanskrit poem*

## Questions/Exercises:

1.  What was the reoccurring thing you were disciplined for as a child?

2.  What if your favorite thing to do?

3.  What are your most destructive habits?

4.  What is your best practice time?

# Chapter 6

# *Salambas*

## Supporters and Friends

*"And this road is full of foot prints!*
*Companions have come before.*
*They are your ladder.*
*Use them!*
*Without them you won't have the spirit quickness*
*you need. Even a dumb donkey*
*crossing a desert becomes nimble footed*
*with others of its kind.*
*Stay with the caravan. By yourself*
*you'll get a hundred times more tired*
*and fall behind."*

Rumi

From the minute you are born, till the minute you die, you need supporters. In the beginning when you are a baby, you will die if you don't have someone to care for you. Throughout your life you usually have family and friends around you who are necessary for your wellbeing. These are important people throughout your journey. When you are starting to dig the well, you will need to support the walls to stop them from falling in. In the Garden plants often need support and need the support of the gardener to create the right conditions for growth. According to E.O. Wilson, Humans are tribal animals who enjoy gathering in groups for special occasions or events. Thanksgiving is one of the gatherings where you show your gratitude for family and friends. You're thankful for them and all your blessings. You live in a society that has so much that you forget how important daily gratitude is for the basic things of life: food, water, shelter, and clothing. You live dependent upon a host of people you don't know to support your daily life. Remember how many people are there behind these things. Do you take all this for granted or do you occasionally think about it?

In this endeavor the support of others is most rewarding. You hope your family and friends will encourage you in this venture, but as you grow, your relationships to family and friends may change. Not everybody is interested in self-study. Many people are content to enjoy life living event to event without self-reflection. Rather than withdrawing from your daily life, let your inner discoveries enhance it. You find comfort in the company of others who understand life as you do and are interested in the same things. In fact it is important to make new friends with these people and also those who are working with the same teacher or mentor. You are creating your own new community.

In the beginning, your teachers and mentors are the most important supporters; they help you put your feet on the right path. When you meet your teacher be like a baby bird, open your mouth and receive the wisdom. Then it is up to you to chew it, swallow and digest it, keeping what is good for you and letting go of the rest. Eventually you will not be able to follow all of their advice, because you will become your own Bible.

Every group has its buzz words. Your salambas should be people who understand what you are doing and speak the same language. When a really good old friend comes into your life, perhaps after a long absence, you are able to share your deepest feelings, joys, and difficulties with them. A true friend will provide support by advising you when they see you are losing your direction.

You are refining yourself. If your life is becoming different from others you may feel isolated and maybe strange. You are not one of the crowd any more: your vision has broadened to include more subtle aspects.

For more information on BKS Iyengar, please visit: http://bksiyengar.com

I had the rich gift of studying Pantanjalis Yoga personally with B.K.S. Ivengar. Both in Puna, India and in the United States from 1974.

For more information on Swami Shivanada Radha, please visit: www.yasodhara.org/swami-radha

Swami Shivanada Radha was also a very important teacher for me. I lived at the Yasodhara Ashram in Canada for three years.

They were two wonderful teachers who were interested in seeing me develop my potential and encouraged me to take action to bring it into fruition. Sometimes they appeared less than gentle, but they were truthful and I came to understand that compassion often is tough love. They saw the mistake I was making at that time and gave me courage to change. I have familiar knots and tangles in my body and psyche and these are what I need to recognize and clarify. Friends and teachers often give me constructive criticism on my behavior from a vantage point I am blind to, allowing me to see myself with more clarity.

B.K.S. Iyengar, my spiritual father, was my root teacher. I met him in 1974 after practicing yoga for 12 years. Through Shri Iyengar's teaching I learned about the temple of my body and how to use it ethically and I began my journey into my psyche. He was the most benevolent person I have ever met. He saw my potential and demanded I give 110% to reach it.

I understood more and more how his wisdom was that the body is the most manifest aspect of ourselves and in some ways the easiest layer in which to create awareness and change. Memories are actually embodied and they can be brought to consciousness by physical exploration linked with awareness and concentration. B.K.S. Iyengar was the most inspiring example of this; without fail he practiced every day until he died at 95. He was the author of many Yoga books, all of which have the word "Light" in their title. His most important books are Light on Yoga, and Light on Life.

I went to Yasodhara Ashram in 1981 after leaving my family and worked with Swami Radha, my spiritual mother. She was a great teacher and author/creator of "Kundalini Yoga for the

West" an explanation of the pictorial journey of the Chakra System. The Chakra System is teachings from very ancient times and the symbolism of the pictures had been partly lost. She reinterpreted these pictorial representations of the characteristics that are invaluable to investigate on a journey of the discovery of ourselves. She taught me how to be rigorously honest with myself and how to use my mind and intelligence to find my inner teacher.

She taught me that hunches and insights that we follow are evidence of increased sensitivity and when pursued will lead to a high degree of perception. She told very clever stories, like parables, about various people and her interaction with them. Her stories included powerful, subtle messages. It was my job to pay attention deeply and hear how what she was saying applied to me. If I wasn't listening or aware, the teaching went over my head and was lost.

Both of these people were totally sincere, honest, ethical and admirable and are the main point of reference in my life. Sometimes it appeared as if they were being unkind. But they held true to their vision of my potential, never backing away, but always demanding the best from me. I now know this as the deepest form of compassion.

Your journey is uniquely your own and not exactly like your teacher's. Swami Radha suggested you always try to see three possible outcomes. Your own perception of outcomes is often tunnel vision, and being in a sharing group offers other people's vision which then broadens your own, allowing you to redirect your thinking without destroying your enthusiasm. Sometimes you are attached to a certain outcome and don't see the trap you have set for yourself. You always have to be aware of the misleading trickiness of your ego. If you discuss these things with your friends they can sometimes point out your mistakes and refocus you.

When someone criticizes you, don't immediately defend yourself, just listen and consider if what they say has truth in it. You may need time to clarify your own sense of self. If you find what they've said does have truth for you, then you have work to do. Those times when there is no truth in it and it is that person's opinion just let it run off your back like water off a duck's back. This was advice from Swami Radha. I experienced this test many times with Swami Radha. If she criticized you wrongly and you defended yourself, you had failed the test. The lesson she was helping me learn was that other people's opinions are only that, if it's not true for me it is simply their opinion. This helped me to have a better idea of my boundaries of who I knew I was.

In California in the 70s along with my practice of yoga I belonged to a Women's Consciousness Raising Group. There were about 10 of us. We took turns at being the leader, introducing some idea that we really knew nothing about and experimenting. Often it was listening to music, drawing, doing visualization and then sharing what we discovered about ourselves from these exercises.

One day we decided to try an exercise of pretending we were going to die in three months. We discussed what we would want to do with our last remaining three months. As I was in a very happy phase of my life and felt content I was the one who was chosen to "die" first. We had decided on an open coffin ceremony. My Salambas sat around the coffin which was made of couch pillows. Out loud, I expressed what I thought would be the feeling of dying, how the cold began in my feet and spread upward to my legs and then throughout my entire body. I then practiced Shavasana which is Corpse Pose, a Yoga practice of relaxation of the body and a quietening of the mind. This is a practice that is done at the end of every Yoga session. It is an important aspect of life to be able to relax and feel peaceful. So there I am, feeling calm and relaxed while my Salambas discussed me, my life, and how sad they were that I had died. As if my death were true, one of the participants broke into tears and started sobbing. I continued to feel very relaxed and comfortable. In the moment, this experience of "death" felt real and I recognized how content I was with my life. I thought about the only thing I had said I still wanted to do, which was to restore my friendship with my sister. As my one friend continued to sob I began to feel anxious for her and decided to "come back to life". She rushed out of the room still sobbing, and when she came back, told us how terrified she was of dying. We were then able to discuss our individual and collective ideas about death and dying. I know now that intellectually, I have no fear of death. Of course this may change when I am faced with the real thing.

The added surprise was that when I got home my two year old son told me he had a birthday present for me. Although it wasn't actually my birthday, he had chosen a scarf at the nursery school that morning out of the lost and found bin. Here I had just "died" and here is my little boy presenting me with a birthday present. To this day, the universe playing tricks like that makes me laugh and be grateful!

I had begun to question the patterns I grew up with. My mother's example was of wife and mother. I felt there were many other areas which interested me as well. I knew there was a lot I didn't know about myself and these were my extracurricular interests. While my children were small I spent 13 years being a devoted mother. It was only when the youngest went to kindergarten that I truly felt I could take some time to explore the other aspects of myself.

The day my youngest son went to kindergarten was like any other. That night when my husband and I went to bed I realized life was into a new phase. I gave a big sigh and said, "Now I can think about what I want to do." His answer was, "Let's have another baby." I said, "No way!"

When my boys were in their late teen years, I told them that I would always be their Mother and would love them, but I no longer needed to mother them. They were now young men exploring life for themselves.

Gratitude and recognition are the appropriate responses to your Salambas. They are the teachers and people that have encouraged you in your venture. Who have helped you verify that your garden is blooming and the waters of the spirit are flowing. Your metamorphosis into a more aware and conscious being are the indicators from outside that validate your growing authenticity. This will continue with your commitment to daily practice and the help and support of many people around you.

## *Questions/Exercises:*

1. Do you have a friend with whom you can share your deepest thought and feelings?

2. Are you able to be yourself even if you feel you are not one of the group?

3. Do you think of your gratitudes every night?

# Chapter 7

# Harvest

*It is the height of absurdity to sow only weeds in the first half of one's lifetime and expect to harvest a valuable crop in the second half.*

Percy Johnston

Harvest time is when you gather the benefits of the growing season. If you had planted a fruit tree in your garden and watered it and pruned it at the right time, you would now be gathering the fruit. This is the analogy for you if you have been practicing regularly and facing your challenges. Take a look back at your life before you started on this adventure. Looking at yourself have the qualities of gratitude, forgiveness, humility, patience, fearlessness, faith and contentment changed. They are all the fruits of your harvest. As far as anger and fear are a part of life for most of us are you able to soften your response and let go more readily?

Your Harvest may not all come at the same time, but may be the recognition of random small rewards that show you that you have evolved. You are a better and happier human being -- being more in the present and able to be less upset by what appear to be negative happenings. Your mind is making decisions more clearly, and you are able to live with more equanimity. Faith, contentment and maturity are the rich soil of a well-tended garden. Like a garden, there are areas of yourself that are perennial that continue to need regular attention. And then there are the aspects of your life that are more like the annuals that come and go. Your garden is never finished; remember to stay aware of the continual changes. The art of living a contented life is to accept changes and challenges with faith in your ability to flow with all that life brings—this is maturity.

Look into the basket of your Harvest and see the healthy yields of your practice.

*Gratitude* is a feeling that makes you want to say "thank you".

Gratitude and forgiveness are the wisdom practices of the heart; they release the generosity of spirit and open the doors of healing. If you are grateful, then your heart is at peace. Gratitude is an appreciation that something has been done for you by someone or that an event in your life has occurred that has made your heart understand that all is well. We often take the essentials -- food, clothing, and shelter-- for granted. We forget how much these are things to be grateful for. There is a Sufi sect that 'thanks' everything that they consume or use by kissing it.

An experience I had in India made me realize that in our society we have so much to be grateful for --and yet we expect so much more. My experience there opened my eyes to the small 'gratitude's' in my life that I should be grateful for; I have food, clothing, and shelter, friends and support, and my health.

My sister in law who lived in India for several years told me on my first visit never to give money to children because they were being used by adult pimps. She said to carry fruit and offer it to them if they looked hungry.

On my daily walk to class I passed the same family every day. They lived on the street and had a little boy about five who was very dark and never had a stitch of clothing on him. One day as I passed he looked at me and with a cheeky smile held out his hand. I had a lovely golden orange and gave it to him. He danced down the road holding the orange up in both of his hands like an offering to the sun. This brought beautiful wonderful feelings of joy and gratitude to my heart. When I returned to Palo Alto, California, after a month in India, I told my husband I had seen more miserable faces in a week in California than during my entire time in India.

*Forgiveness* is taking the actions that allow you to let go of your negative emotional attachment to an incident.

Forgiveness does not necessarily mean forgetting. Forgiveness is freedom from attachment to the pain of an experience; you know you have forgiven when you stop suffering. However don't forget the valuable lessons inherent in the experience.

When I divorced my husband my in-laws were very angry with me and cut off all communication. I understood their loyalty but as I thought about it I felt my feelings towards them had not changed. I continued to send them birthday cards with news and greetings and at Christmas a newsy letter about the boys. After three years I got a long letter from them apologizing for their abrupt attitude towards me and thanked me for keeping in touch with them. I felt it was time to visit South Africa to meet with them again. This was a very rewarding visit. Making the journey cemented our love and mutual forgiveness.

My father in-law died three months later. This was a very important lesson I learnt. If you have older relatives, as much as you can complete the cycle of love and forgiveness before they die. Grieving is about the things you never said or never did. And now they have died and you are left with your regrets.

In the ups and downs of relationships, the other person may not even know you are upset and so you are creating suffering for yourself. Seldom do you know the person's inner landscape or motivation.

Have you forgiven yourself for actions in the past that created suffering for yourself and others? Have you looked for forgiveness -- have you made what reparations are possible by speaking, writing, or communicating in some way? In 20/20 hindsight, do you now have a present awareness of these actions for which you are asking forgiveness? Forgiving yourself is the first step and then you will forgive others who transgress. Asking forgiveness allows you to live in the present and not be caught in your past.

*"Be non-attached to past suffering. Be sure to learn from it."*

Swaim Radha

*Humility* shows the understanding that your ego is not the center of the world.

You have awareness that there are many ways to live life and it is every person's choice. Ego is necessary to have a presence in the world; ego is a good servant, but a bad master. Humility is a deep feeling that, along with awareness, helps you to stop slipping back into delusions about yourself. Study yourself and your actions and be ruthlessly honest.

*Patience* is a mature characteristic, but you have to be careful.

Patience comes when you don't react immediately but you bring the light of awareness to yourself and examine your outward behaviors and inwardly examine your thoughts. Patience is a facet of being true to yourself and allows you to have understanding and tolerance for differences.

What you are considering to be patience may actually be procrastination. Both these words mean not to act, but there is a fine line between patience and procrastination. Procrastination often brings feelings of guilt. You know you should do it, but something holds you back—what is that something? Can you name the resistance?

*Anger* has two faces.

There is righteous anger that will come up spontaneously in a situation where your feeling can be expressed and then you let it go. And there is unrighteous anger that is not expressed, which gets tucked away and is allowed to simmer and creates resentment and suffering. This is the type of anger I worked on at the ashram in the story shared in Chapter 4: Communication. You are not perfect, but none of us is. It is the human condition. There will still be times when the negative emotions of anger arise. We all have to live with ourselves and should never do anything that would make you not like yourself.

When I was a child I had a bad temper, what I now call a "red temper." I totally lost my awareness in it and didn't know what I was doing. Afterwards I would feel ashamed and not happy with myself. One day I became present as I was beating on my small brother and realized how wrong this was. Slowly I became more aware and was able to pick up the warning signs before I lost myself in the anger. I learnt to express my anger verbally rather than physically. The Harvest for me was realizing that being happy with myself was much more important than allowing myself to lose my temper.

Sometimes it is not suitable to express your anger immediately, but it is important at a later time to speak to the person about what you felt.

*"Suffering is the mental continuation of pain."* Vimala Thakar

*Fear* is another emotion that we might call negative but it is one that keeps us safe.

We react very quickly to a physical threat and that is as it should be. Mental fears however need to be looked at carefully to see what basis they have in reality.

My fear has always been of falling. I lived my life never going near the edge of anything. I've also always been really careful when coming down the stairs or a mountain. The time in Nepal made me face this fear over and over again, until I realized this fear was in my hard wiring. I had to recognize it and then proceed.

In Nepal, when we were 17,000ft up and had to come down a 500ft hill, one of the Sherpas grabbed my hand and started running. I had no time to think of my fear and ran freely all the way down with him! This was a very freeing experience and taught me—don't think—just do.

*"Thought breeds fear."* Krishnamurti

Other mental fears are usually in our imagination or in our dreams. In dream life they take on the appearance of something you are afraid of that may be chasing you, or threatening to kill you. You can work on this in your conscious work on dreams. What is chasing you in your life that you are afraid of? Fears in your conscious mind also need facing and inquiring if they have any basis in reality. Are they your mind that you are using negatively instead of positively? Remember it is your thinking that creates this fear. For instance when someone doesn't come home at the time you expect them your mind brings up all the worst scenarios.

How many times have you spent your mental energy fearing an event, only to find out it wasn't that bad or was even enjoyable? You don't know what the future holds. So it is better to bring yourself to your body. Take a deep breath, so you can focus on what is happening in the present. Fears are thoughts that limit us. You need courage to face them using your practice to bolster your trust in life and its purpose, which is to evolve. Each fear that you face and conquer will give you more freedom. If you keep your spirit young with a sense of adventure, accepting challenges and maintaining a vital interest in people and in the world, your life will develop into one of humility and contentment.

### *"Take an affirmative stance towards life."* Huston Smith

Your deep fears and angers are a mystery where they come from. They seem to be an inherent part of us. They are the demons that we have to learn to face during our life. As you become aware of them and as you face them we can transform them into knowledge about yourself and therefor have control over these negative inborn emotions.

*Faith* is a set of values and prejudices which color your perceptions, governs your thinking, and dictates your responses.

As a child you live with adults who bring you up with their belief system. It shapes your life without you being aware of its presence or power. When you become mature with effort and awareness, you can choose what you trust. If you feel yourself in acute discomfort and don't understand why, question it.

### *"It is good not to feel well-adjusted in a wrong situation."* Gandhi

Life offers you opportunities to grow and you may have to shed the belief system you grew up with. This occurs when you have the courage to decide for yourself. Belief systems by their very nature can be limiting. You can stay small and live constricted or be like a snake and shed the old skin as you grow.

I grew up with a mother and father who never got divorced and lived a happy and content married life. When I got married this was my belief system: that I married for life. I tried to live my parent's story, to stay within the marriage. My husband had influenced me so much that I felt I never had the opportunity to get to know myself. For years I had supported him in his crusade in crossdressing. But, I was finding it more and more difficult to live with him and his choice that had so dramatically changed him and challenged my more traditional thinking. His crossdressing created feelings of intense frustration and embarrassment in not being able to live in a way that was comfortable to me. I was able to tolerate the dichotomy for the years it took for my boys to grow up. Then, I chose leave the relationship. This took courage to face the feelings of guilt and disappointment of not fulfilling my young dream of being "married for life". Now, knowing myself had become my driving desire.

Sharon Salzburg differentiates between "bright faith", that which we have in our teacher or mentor, and "inner faith", which develops from your own authority (you become your own bible). Begin to pay attention to whose voice you're following. When there is uncertainty, without surety, which faith is sustaining you, your teacher's "bright faith" or your "inner faith"? Both are valuable and knowing which you are following is maturity. When we have the faith to take a step it is like planting seeds in the garden, then doing your homework, like watering, and then having faith that they will germinate and grow. You are living your life in accordance with your belief system. You walk your talk.

*"We all have to have a belief system
to function, but construct it
on a bamboo frame;
don't set it in concrete, so it can
easily be changed as you grow in wisdom."*
Swami Radha

*Contentment* is a feeling of the moment. It is not complacency.

It is when you are aware in the moment doing something that pleases you. You can even feel content if it is an effort that you know will lead to a good end. You live with yourself and hopefully will become your own best friend.

Never do anything that would make you not like yourself, or if you do, make reparations as soon as you can.

Heroes and heroines believe that they have a contribution to make to the world. Steven Hawking who was diagnosed with ALS at an early age lost the use of his body slowly, and has continued to keep his brilliant mind active. Because of his courage and willingness to face his physical deterioration we have the great benefit of knowing a lot more about our universe.

*No matter what we encounter in life it is faith that enables us to try again, trust again, and to love again."* The Buddha

*Maturity* is the recognition that there is a power other than yourself and that life does not revolve around you.

With maturity you have developed a sense of trust in the universe and yourself. It's not that negative-appearing obstacles don't come up, but that you have developed a much more philosophical approach. You are able to take what action is necessary in the situation and accept the outcome. Without action it becomes complacency which is a dead feeling that you are helpless. Do what you can do and then relax.

When we recognize a power greater than ourselves, we are able to accept the vicissitudes of life, experiencing equanimity, neither getting too excited when things are going well or too depressed when they appear not to be flowing easily. Pain and pleasure are life, but we don't need to suffer.

### *Maturity is achieved when a person postpones immediate pleasures for long-term values.*

Even in times of immense difficulty it is faith that enables us to relate to the present moment in such a way that we can go forward instead of becoming lost in resignation or despair. Faith links our present day experience—whether wonderful or terrible—to the underlying pulse of life itself that is change.

Faith and courage are the combined qualities you need to take the first steps; to see the unknown as an adventure, to launch a journey into yourself. While you are alive, this journey never ends, as the truth is that we are always changing and need to stay aware and in the present.

## INDIAN STORY ABOUT
## THE BEGINNING OF THE WORLD

This is a story I heard in India. In the beginning of time the Divine Spirit lived on the earth with humans. Human beings are very curious, and asked endless questions. After millions of years the Spirit, tired of all the questions, asked the wise council to suggest where to hide. They first suggested, "Go to the highest mountain." Spirit said, "No, they will get there. Think again." So they suggested, "Go and live at the bottom of the deepest ocean." "No they will get there too." "Think again." At long last the council said, "Hide your divinity deep in the center of their own being, for humans will never think to look for it there." All agreed that this was the perfect hiding place, and the deed was done. And since that time humans have been going up and down the earth, digging, diving, climbing, and exploring--searching for something already within themselves.

# Book List

Light on Yoga by B.K.S. Iyengar

Tree of Yoga by B.K.S. Iyengar

Light on Life by B.K.S. Iyengar

Kundalini Yoga for the West Swami Shivananda Radha

The Wisdom of Patanjali's Yoga Sutras by Ravi Ravindra

One Handed Basket Weaving (Rumi)
Translated by Coleman Barks

The Kabir Book (Kabir) Translated by Robert Bly

Faith by Sharon Salzburg

Start Where You Are by Pema Chodron

Second Half of Life by Angeles Arrien

The Way Things Are by Huston Smith

*"I'm not Aging,*

*I'm Evolving."*

Felicity in her Garden May 2016

*Blessings on your journey.*

FelicityGreenYoga.com

CPSIA information can be obtained
at www.ICGtesting.com
Printed in the USA
FSOW03n2218271117
41732FS